KURLEY
For President

KURLEY
For President

★★★★★★★★★★★★★★★★★★★★★★★★★

A Politically Incorrect
Book on Politics

J. A. Harter

iUniverse

KURLEY FOR PRESIDENT
A Politically Incorrect Book on Politics

iUniverse books may be ordered through booksellers or by contacting:

iUniverse
1663 Liberty Drive
Bloomington, IN 47403
www.iuniverse.com
1-800-Authors (1-800-288-4677)

Because of the dynamic nature of the Internet, any web addresses or links contained in this book may have changed since publication and may no longer be valid. The views expressed in this work are solely those of the author and do not necessarily reflect the views of the publisher, and the publisher hereby disclaims any responsibility for them.

Any people depicted in stock imagery provided by Thinkstock are models, and such images are being used for illustrative purposes only. Certain stock imagery © Thinkstock.

ISBN: 978-1-4917-7639-1 (sc)
ISBN: 978-1-4917-7640-7 (e)

Print information available on the last page.

iUniverse rev. date: 10/12/2015

A Laugh A Minute

A Politically "Incorrect" Book
by Kurley
Knoodle
Book

Kurley for President

~

by Kurley Knoodle

© J. Harter

Kate Knoodle
from
Knoodle Hdqtrs.

Kurley Knoodle

Speaking of Poli"tiks"

A question and answer book about some of today's pressing politi"kal" issues, answered for you by Kurley Knoodle one of the newest Presidential Hopefuls speaking to you direct from Knoodle Headquarters in Knoodle World, USA

The Reporter

A Laugh a Minute
with
Kurley Knoodle
On Line

For Presidents.....World Leaders....
Politicians.....Democrats....Republicans....the
Armed Forces.........and just People in general
who like to have a good laugh at our World
and its poli"tiks".

 From Kurley Knoodle

VIP List

Complimentary
Autographed
Copies are being
sent to the following
dignitaries

1. President Obama
2. V. P. Joe Biden
3. Hilary Clinton
4. George W. Bush
5. Governor Christie of New Jersey
6. Donald Trump
7. Japanese Real Estate Broker
8. and many more

from
Knoodle Headquarters
USA

Kurley Knoodle
On Line

America
"Plugged in"

www.kurleyonline.
aol.com
Dateline: USA

Kurley Knoodle
is (The newest
presidential
candidate) to throw
his hat into the ring
as he goes on the
worldwide web and
offers "Comic Relief"
to the country.

Kurley says: "In this world where people are
stressed out about poli"tiks", their HMO's,
PPO's and CEO's he is offering "Comic
Relief" with a politikally Incorrect "Knoodle
Joke" Book With Kate and Kurley "Speaking
Of Poli"tiks".

Action Backstage:

Kurley and Kate are getting ready for their first national television show. Make-up people are putting the final touches on hair, make-up, etc.

Kurley: *Is my tin-hat on straight? (Note: Kurley wears a silver tin-pot on his head).*

Kate: *That's your Presidential hat?*

Kurley: *Sure - this is the latest style for Presidential candidates - in case anyone wants to throw rocks.*

You never knoweth who wanted to throweth the first stoneth........

Footnote: *Kate is the serious one and Kurley is fun and carefree. Kate interviews Kurley on all kinds of Presidential questions and is mostly exasperated at his answers.*

Kate Knoodle
from
Knoodle Hdqtrs.

Press Release
Knoodle Headquarters,
Knoodle World, USA

It is <u>not official</u> yet....that Kurley Knoodle is Running for President. Knoodle Headquarters is waiting for an official, official announcement from some official. But in this off-election year Kurley Knoodle is making some profound statements on government and world affairs....that are certain to go down in history. Example ....

Question: Kurley, what do you think of the shrinking of the dollar bill.

Answer:....They should <u>Pre-Shrink It!</u>

Kate Knoodle, Reporter

Question

Kurley, what would you do about the shrinking of the dollar bill??

The shrinking of the dollar bill?

Kurley

Pre-shrink it!

KATE
KNOODLE

from

KNOODLE HDQTRS.

Kate Knoodle
from
Knoodle Hdqtrs.

Question: What is the highest award the government can give to an individual?

Answer: ...A tax refund check

****

Reporter

Kurley, what do you think of tax collecting?

Kurley

I'm in to Stamp collecting myself.

Reporter

What do you think of the Premier cabinet post?

Kurley

I think it would look better
if they waxed and polished it
then painted it green.

Question: Kurley, since you are running for president have you had any psychological testing or brain testing?

Answer: Yes, I have. I've heard that anyone who runs for president should have his head examined.

Question: What did they find from testing your brain?

Answer: Nothing!

Kurley: I am completely gluten – free, suger - free, salt- free, brain- free, so I should be the perfect candidate for president

- - - - -

Q.   Kurley.....what made you run for president?

A.   The Devil made me do it!!

KATE from KNOODLE HDQTRS.

Kate Knoodle

Speaking of Poli"tiks"

Reporter: Kurley, what about your policy with North America?

Kurley: I don't have a policy with North America......I have a policy with New York Life!

Kurley Knoodle

Question: What do you think of the Internal Revenue Service

Answer: I think the IRS has given us enough service for awhile. They are overworked and overpaid. I think we should give them the next ten years off....or a permanent vacation!

Kurley Knoodle

Public

Affairs

?

Question: What do you think of Public
            affairs?

Answer:..Oh is the public having affairs?
          I just hope they keep their public
          affairs private.

Reporter

How many judges would you put on the bench?

Kurley

About nine, but I think they would be more comfortable on the couch.

****

Reporter

What do you think of women in government?

Kurley

They make good governors cause they sure know how to govern their husbands.

Question: Kurley, what do you think they
should do about the shrinking of
the dollar bill?

Answer: They should pre-shrink it?

Reporter

I just read that joke and saw that dollar on
the first page.

Kurley

I know. I'm letting you take a good look at it
before they shrink it again.

Reporter

Kurley, who would you have running your foreign affairs?

Kurley

Foreigners!

****

Reporter

What of the famine in Ethiopia?

Kurley

Oh! Is the famine loose again? I thought they caught him a long time ago.

****

Reporter

What about Guatemala?

Kurley

I love Guatemala. It is my favorite dip.

Q. Kurley, what is the biggest decision that the American people have to make on a daily basis?

A. Well, Kate, everyday when they go to the market they have a big decision to make....... Will it be *paper or plastic*!!!

Question: Kurley, what do you think of the
FBI and CIA?

Answer: Personally, I prefer the NFL
and NBA

****

Kurley Knoodle

The
NFL?
and
NBA?

<u>Reporter</u>

What about the Bears in Chicago?

<u>Kurley</u>

Set bear traps!

****

Bear-traps?

Reporter

Kurley, what do you think
is the biggest problem our
country faces today?

Kurley

Well Sir, we have Bears in Chicago...Rams
in St. Louis.. Lions in Detroit.. And Buffalo in
New York. I think what our country needs is
better animal control.

Kurley Knoodle

Bears
Rams
Lions
Buffalo

*What this country
needs is better
animal control.*

Kate Knoodle
from
Knoodle Hdqtrs.

Kurley Knoodle

Reporter

Kurley, do you plan to do anything Religious for the country?

Kurley

Yes I do. The first religious thing I am going to do is to take-up a collection.

A collection?

Kate Knoodle

Speaking of Poli"tiks"

Reporter: Kurley, what about your policy
with North America?

Kurley: I don't have a policy with North
America......I have a policy
with New York life!

Kurley Knoodle

Kate Knoodle

****

Reporter

Do you think we should send a of our Aides to other countries?

Kurley

No! Other countries already have their own aides. We would just be aiding to their problems?

Reporter

Speaking of Aides, Kurley, who would be your top Aides?

Kurley

I have three Knoodle-Aides.

Fuzzy, Bugsy, and Skuzzy

Fuzzy is my right hand-man

"SKUZZY" KNOODLE

Skuzzy is my middle-man

Bugsy is my left hand-man

Kurley's left hand-man

Fuzzy Knoodle

Skuzzy

Bugsy

Reporter

Can you let us in on what these executives are going to be doing?

Kurley

It is still a little fuzzy as to what Fuzzy is going to be doing as yet, but I am sure it will become clear pretty soon.

"Skuzzy" Knoodle

Skuzzy is in-charge of keeping the government Klean

Bugsy is my kampaign manager

And my entertainment director

Reporter

Kurley, do you have a party?

Kurley

We are always having a party.

Reporter

What is the name of your party?

Kurley

The Kompassionate Party

Bugsy helped organize our "Kompassionate Party"

Party Poli"tiks"

Reporter

Now the Big Question, Kurley. We have Socialism & Capitalism.... What is Knoodle-ism?

Kurley

Knoodle-ism is being kind and Kompassionate to others.

Our motto is:

"Be kind and kompassionate - throw a party for others"

I tip my hat to
"Knoodle-ism"

Question:

Kurley, how do you plan to preserve wildlife?

Answer:

Throw a party

Preserve wildlife
Throw a party

Kurley Knoodle

Issues?

<u>Reporter</u>

Kurley, let's get back to the issues? There's been enough knoodlin' goin on!

<u>Kurley</u>

Of course, let's get back to the issues.... issues ....issues.....

I like Knoodlin' better!

Don't let <u>anything</u> stop you!

Reporter

Kurley, what about the Senate Race?

Kurley

Oh! Are the senators having a race? I will have to look into that. Where are they racing?

The senate race?

<u>Reporter</u>

Kurley, what kind of Speakers would you get for the House?

<u>Kurley</u>

Probably RCA, Emerson or Magnavox

****

House Speakers?

RCA .... Emerson .....or Magnavox ?????

Reporter

Somehow, Kurley, all your answers seem to bring up another question

All your answers seem to be answer-errors .....

Kurley

That is because all your questions are question-errors!

Reporter

All in all, Kurley, you seem a liile bit Fuzzy on some of these guestions.

Kurley

No. I think you are a little confused. I'm not Fuzzy .... I'm Kurley..............

Question:

What about nuclear power? How would you handle it?

Answer:

Very karefully!

Question:

What kind of power are you in favor of?

Answer:

Knoodle power

Knoodle power

Knoodle power

is the power to show kindness, Kompassion and Klove to others!!

Reporter:

How would you show kindness and Kompassion to your veteran?

Kurley:

I would have a

Hug your Veteran Day!

<u>Reporter</u>

Maybe Kurley is not so Fuzzy afterall.

Kurley

I'm not Fuzzy
I'm Kurley

Reporter

What about the movements of the military?

Kurley

I understand the military makes some excellent moves especially when they are off-duty. I heard that is when they make all the right moves!

Reporter: How are we going to get the Navy Boys back on the Farm?

Kurley: Easy.....put a girl on every farm!!

Question: How does an Army boy spell relief?

Answer: McDonald's

XXXXXX

Question: How would you improve the food in the Army?

Answer: Bring in a new chef!

Question: Who would that be?

Answer: Kol. Sanders

Question: How are we going to get rid of the marine - layer in the country?

Answer: Bring in the Army. Let them lay around for awhile.

Kate Knoodle

Reporter

Kurley, what do you think about women's Rights?

Kurley

I'm for any woman that is right.

Kurley:

The only trouble is finding the right women!

Do you have a solution to this problem?

Kurley:

Yes! The first thing I would do is form three groups. I would form a Men's Rights Group, a Women's Wrong Group and a Men's Wrong Group...... This way we will get the right women together with the right men....and the wrong women together with the wrong men.

This should solve that problem!!

Reporter

What do you think about Daylight Savings Time?

Kurley

I am in favor of saving time both day and night. Maybe we should go on Nighttime Savings Time too.

(Oh, Kurley, where do you think these up?)

Nighttime savings??

Reporter

Kurley, What would you advise the country to invest in .... soy beans, wheat or Pork bellies?

Kurley

Moth balls

Reporter

Moth balls! Why moth balls?

Kurley

Because I heard that the last time they opened the door to the treasury - that all that came out were Moths because, the only thing in the treasury was Paper Money.

Moth balls?

So moth balls are your best investment.

Kate Knoodle

Reporter: What do you think the second best investment would be?

Kurley: Golf balls

Reporter: Why golf balls?

Kurley: Because all the Japanese are taking up golf. So there will probably be a run on golf balls!!

Answer: Yes, Kate. We now have a new
           Ball Market!

Money market ... Bull
market ..... Bear market

"Ball market"

Reporter: What would be the best way to defeat the enemy?

Kurley: Feed them army food!

XXXXXXXX

Reporter: Why are the marines so smart?

Kurley: They eat marine food!

Reporter

Do you believe in good food and jogging?

Kurley

Yes, I jog everyday.

Reporter

Where do you jog?

Kurley

I jog everyday down to the donut shop.

Reporter

What would you do about crime in the streets?

Kurley

I would take it out of the streets and put it on the freeways. I don't think anything could survive there!

("Kurley has a solution for everything")
????

Reporter

Do you think we are too soft on criminals?

Kurley

Yes! But the jury is still hung-up on that.....
and as usual, instead of hanging
the criminal.....they hung the
jury!

Reporter

What do you think of people who go for Chapter 13?

Kurley

More power to them. I can never get beyond Chapter Two before I fall asleep.

Reporter

What do you of the political scene?

Kurley

I don't like scenes at all. I think that scenes should be avoided at all costs.

Q. Kurley..... have you had any formal education? Are you a Harvard or Yale man?

A. I guess you would call me a "Knocks" man because I've been through the school of Hard Knocks.

Q. What was your major?

A. Knocking

****

Kurley ....I kept Knock, knock, knocking on Hollywood doors .... but no one would answer. I wanted to become an actor.

Kurley Knoodle
On Line

AMERICA
"Plugged In"

Since I couldn't get into Hollywood I decided to go to Washington D.C. I heard they have some real good actors up there.

****

Kurley 'K'

A Laugh a Minute
with
Kurley Knoodle
On Line

Speaking of Poli "tiks"

****

Q.   Has the Obama administration uncovered the secrets of weapons and mass destruction?

A.   Kurley---Yes!

Q.   What is that?

A.   The School Lunch Program

****

A Laugh a Minute
with
Kurley Knoodle
On Line

Q. Kurley--- Have you ever had an Obama Burger!

Kate --- No!

Kurley --- Well after you had an Obama Burger -- you have to run straight for the nearest bathroom.

Reporter

Kurley, have you thought yet as to where we can send the IRS on their vacation?

Kurley

Yes! Clud Fed for a Permanent Vacation!!

Club Fed

Club
Fed
?

For a permanent
vacation!

Reporter

Do you think they have any smart men
working in central intelligence?

Central Intelligence???

Kurley

No, because if they were smart they wouldn't be working at all!

A Laugh a Minute
with
Kurley Knoodle
On Line

Q. Why do you think Mitt Romney didn't
run for a 3rd time?

A. He probably didn't think that the 3rd
time would be a charm

****

Q. What's the last thing Ronald Reagan
said to George Bush as he was taking
over the White House?

A. --- "Let George do it"!

Q. Kurley .... How would you support women's groups who want to support a woman for president --- such as Hilary Clinton?

A. I'd wear Support Hose

****

Q. What about Huckabee? Do you think he would fit into the oval office?

A. I don't know. Some people think he is a "little square" so I don't know if he'd fit into the oval office.

Keeping up with The Kardashians

Q.   In our pop culture
     world are you
     keeping up with
     The Kardashians

A.   Yes, somewhat! And if
     they wish to support
     me, Kurley "K" for
     president, I will be
     happy to send them
     some support hose!

I will also put in an extra pair for Bruce
Jenner as he is going to need lots of
support!

Kurley "K"

Q. What big news did Bruce Jenner reveal in his TV interview with Diane Sawyer?

A. That he is a Republican!!

A Laugh a Minute
with
Kurley Knoodle
On Line

Q.   Now Kurley ..... about a health plan.
Obama has Obama Care. What would
you call your health Plan

A.   Knoodle Care!!

Everyone needs a little "Knoodle Care"

Reporter

Kurley, why don't they have more Women in the Secret Service?

Kurley

'Cause I heard women....... can't keep a secret.

Reporter

Are you going to have any women in your Secret Service?

Kurley

Yes! Because I don't have any secrets to keep.

Kurley Knoodle

Reporter

What is the biggest secret that the government has?

Kurley

No one knows because, it is such a secret! Not even the government knows!

Reporter

Does the government know who their secret agents are?

Kurley

No! They are all sworn to secrecy so nobody knows.

Secret Service Women

Q.	Do you have any secrets that your administration would want to undercover??

A.	Yes! Two big secrets!!

Q.	What are they?

A.	Mc Donald's secret sauce and Col. Sanders recipe for Kentucky Fried chicken.

Kurley:	These are the secrets that the American public needs to Know.

Kurley "K"

Q. Kurley ..... Who is your favorite comedian?

A. Vladmir Putin of Russa

Q. I didn't know he was a comedian!

A. Oh yes ..... He is a real clown *and likes to clown around with other countries!*

Q. I heard that Vladimir Putin really likes the TV program Dancing with the Stars

A. Yes! And I heard he wants to produce a TV show in Russia ..... called "Dancing with the Czars".

****

Dancing with the Czars!

Speaking of Poli "tiks"

****

Kurley To Kate:

You know every president usually has a swan song he sings as he leaves the White House. This was George W. Bush's song as he left for his horse ranch in Texas ----------

I'm back in the saddle again.
Back where a man is a man
It's nice to be President
But I'd soon be Horse Bent
So I'm back in the
Saddle again!

G.W. Bush

******

Kate: Does that mean that Obama will have a swan song too if he retires to Hawaii?

Kurley: Sure! He'll be singing

"I'm back on my surfboard again!
Back where a man is a man
It's nice to be a President
But I'd sooner be
Boardbent and HELL-BENT
So I'm back on my
Surfboard again!

Barack Obama!

Q. Do You think Donald Trump will make it as president?

A. I don't know! But with all his money I sure hope he'll try to buy the White House before the Japanese buy it *and turn it into a Japanese Pagoda*

The White House
Japanese Pagoda

More laughs
with Kurley and Kate

A Laugh a Minute
with
Kurley Knoodle
On Line

Kate: What are your immediate plans, Kurley?

Kurley: Well, I can't wait to get on the Campaign Trail and meet up with Chris Christie governor of New Jersey! He looks like a tough guy and I'd like to try "arm wrestling" with him.

Kate: You better watch out! He might take you down!

Kurley: I'm not scared. I like living dangerously and life in the fast lane!

Kate: What are you doing right now that is dangerous and fast?

Kurley: I'm running for President!!

****

Do you think that politicians should take a lip-reading course?

It would be a good idea except that there are so many <u>foreign-accents</u> out there that it would be hard to read their lips?

Russian Diplomat....

Can the president read my lips? No...he only lip-reads in English.

Reporter

What is the best course that the Arab and the Israelian people should take?

Kurley

They should all take a course in mind-reading!

Reporter

Why a mind-reading course?

Kurley

If they all take the same mind-reading course then they would all be of one mind!!!!! Maybe the government should offer courses in mind-reading, heart-reading, soul-reading ... Then we would all be of One-Mind, One-Heart and One-Soul.

Kurley Knoodle

Reporter

About the border… If they were to build a border between Mexico and America, who do you think should build the wall?

Kurley

WAL-MART……. They are experienced and have built many walls across America.

Kate

Who do you think should pay for the wall?

Kurley

Donald Trump!!!!!... on a Wal-Mart credit card! He says he is very rich…" Let Donald do it!!

OLAY
OLAY
OLAY

Kate Knoodle

Kurley to Kate:

I heard that if Donald Trump becomes president they won't have to build a wall…… because all the Mexicans will return to Mexico…… Olay!

Kate: Kurley if you win the presidency what is the first thing you are going to do?

Kurley: I'm Going to Disneyland

****

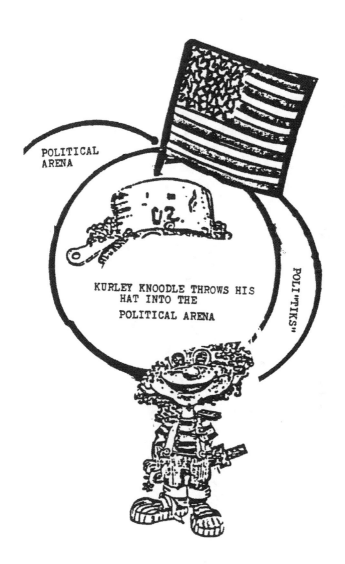

Political Arena

Kurley Knoodle throws his hat
into the political arena

It looks official

Kurley Knoodle
for
President

Keep the kountry straight with Kurley

There's no straighter kandidate than Kurley

Kate Knoodle
from
Knoodle Hdqtrs.

It's Official

Some NFL Official has just made it Official that Kurley Knoodle is the kids kandidate for the presidency. Kurley has just thrown his hat into the politikal arena.

If you care to vote for Kurley or order Kurley's book just write to the address below,

Kurley
Jharter7@cox.net

Have a
Klovable Day
and
Keep on Knoodlin'

Kurley Knoodle

<u>Reporter</u>

What award would you give for peace?

The
    Knobel
            Peace
                    Prize

Kurley Knoodle

Speaking of Poli"tiks"

Kurley for President

Kampaigning for
Kindness
Kourage
Konfidence
Kompassion
and
Klove
throughout the world

Don't forget Kommon Sense and
Kooperation

Kate: Maybe Kurley is not so Fuzzy afterall.

Kurley: I'm not Fuzzy I'm Kurley

Kurley for President
Follow Kurley on Facebook
KURLEY4PRESIDENT@gmail.com

AMERICA
"Plugged in"
www.kurleyonline.
aol.com
Dateline: USA

Kurley Knoodle is (The newest presidential candidate) to throw his hat into the ring as he goes on the worldwide web and offers "Comic Relief" to the country.

Kurley says: "In this world where people are stressed out about poli"tiks", their HMO's, PPO's and CEO's he is offering "Comic Relief" with a politikally incorrect "Knoodle Joke" book with Kate and Kurley "Speaking of Poli"tiks".

A politically "incorrect" book by Kurley Knoodle

Printed in the United States
By Bookmasters